You're a Caregiver, Not a Saint

Yeah, Write!

Lori Ramos Lemasters

You're a Caregiver, Not a Saint: Yeah, Write!
Published by Blue Mercedes Publishing
Littleton, CO

ISBN: 978-0-578-33890-3

SELF-HELP / Journaling

Cover and Interior Design by Victoria Wolf, wolfdesignandmarketing.com. Copyright owned by Lori Ramos Lemasters.

Journal to the Self is both the title of a workshop originally copyrighted and trademarked in 1985, and the title of a book by Kathleen Adams published in 1990 by Warner Books and in continued publication since with Grand Central Publishing. Permission to describe journal techniques from the workshop and/or book is granted by Kathleen Adams, individually and as President of the Center for Journal Therapy, to the author of this work in her role as a certified instructor of the Journal to the Self workshop. Journal to the Self, both book and workshop, are self-help structures intended to teach journal writing techniques and strategies for personal exploration, creative expression and life management. The reliance on Journal to the Self methodologies should not be used in lieu of consultation or advice from licensed medical or behavioral health practitioners.

QUANTITY PURCHASES: Companies, professional groups, clubs, and other organizations may qualify for special terms when ordering quantities of this title. For information, email lori@carepartnersresource.com.

This book is being produced in partnership with Colorado Respite Coalition, a program of Easter Seals Colorado

BLUE MERCEDES
PUBLISHING

*I dedicate this book to my mom and Glenn, without whom
I would not know what it means to be a caregiver.*

*I promised you, Mom, that I would make sure that the lessons
we learned from you surviving your stroke and my subsequent
caregiving journey would be put to good use helping others.*

*Everyday, I feel you both guiding me toward that goal,
and I hope that my work has made you both proud.*

CONTENTS

ACKNOWLEDGMENTS

THANK YOU TO MY SON, Michael, who has always been my heart and has had my back even through the toughest times. You were my rock during my caregiving days and helped me make difficult decisions even when those decisions meant moving twelve hundred miles away from you, Carla, and the kids. I know this was not easy, and yet you put your grandma's well-being above your own feelings and needs. For that, among so many other things, I will always be grateful. God gifted me with you, and I am so grateful.

I also want to thank my daughter-in-law, Carla, for always listening to me and offering sound advice. You have always been my go-to person when I need a level head. I am not sure I could have made it through the whole eight-year caregiving experience and post-grief without the two of you.

I want to thank my grandchildren for your patience and help during those caregiving days. Even though you were so young, you seemed to always understand your great-grandma's needs and gave your grandma (me) much needed comic relief.

HUGE thanks to my brother, the fabulous Gregory Ramos, for your support and expertise and, most importantly, for the time you spent reading, rereading, and editing the earlier versions of this book. Thank God you are a real writer and were able to guide me during the process.

Thank you to my husband, Mike, who came into my life years after my caregiving journey had ended, yet you understand the importance of my work and support it, in spite of your desire to hit the road exploring with no obligations or commitments. I am not sure you realize how much your support and encouragement have meant to me. Thank you for my Christmas gift last year (the financial resources to get this book published). That is the reason we are finally here after nearly ten years, and I am able to check the book off my bucket list.

I would also like to thank the hundreds of caregivers who have attended my self-care classes over the years. Your honesty and willingness to share as we dig into all of the emotions and challenges that we face while caring for a loved one never cease to amaze me. You have taught me so much!

Finally, I want to acknowledge my counselor and mentor, Kathleen Adams, whose guidance and encouragement got me through those difficult years of caring for my parents. It was your belief in me that helped me take the steps to become a certified Journal to the Self® instructor.

INTRODUCTION

As our population continues to age, it is likely that in your lifetime you will either be a caregiver to a family member or friend or be in need of a caregiver yourself.

I became one of the first group in 2001 when my mother, Lupe, survived a stroke while she herself was the primary caregiver for my stepfather, Glenn, who had recently begun dialysis. Reflecting back, I remember the difficult time Mom had in adjusting to her new role. In every conversation, she would talk about how she was struggling to manage getting Glenn to and from dialysis with LA traffic and other obligations. Mom also expressed her concern over Glenn's recent weight loss and lack of energy. I listened to the worry in her voice and wondered how I could help from 1,200 miles away. It never occurred to me that Mom would become ill and that I would take on a pivotal role as caregiver to both my stepdad and her.

You may have been a caregiver; you may currently be a caregiver; or you may see the writing on the wall. No matter where you fall, this book will prepare you for the challenges of caring for a loved one by helping you understand the importance of self-care throughout your caregiving journey.

My goal is to help you realize it's natural and human to feel sad for your loved one and their situation. But it is also reasonable to experience emotions like anger, grief, regret, guilt, and frustration. Human relationships are complex—and even more so concerning people we love. Through this book, you'll develop journaling techniques to help you understand your emotions and manage your responses, perceptions, and actions in the day-to-day management of your role as a caregiver. My hope is that by doing so, you will have a more positive caregiving journey.

My experience with journaling began in 1998, several years before my mom's stroke. I was at a low point in my life, so low in fact, I was questioning whether I even wanted to go on, and I was desperate for help. I opened the yellow pages to counseling and saw a picture of a smiling face. I dialed the number and waited anxiously as it rang. A soft voice answered, "Hello, this is Kathleen Adams." I told her my situation; she cleared her calendar and asked me to come right in to see her. In that moment, my relationship with Kay and Journal to the Self® (JTTS) began. With her guidance, I wrote through divorce, the loss of my birth father, and trying to understand how childhood trauma and grief had framed my adult relationships.

While Mom was in ICU at UCLA Medical Center, I continued to use JTTS techniques, such as list making, which helped me stay organized. I wrote down my questions and the doctors' answers to help keep facts straight. I used my journal to write about my feelings during this frightening time. But when Mom became more stable and moved from ICU to long-term care, the focus turned from wondering if she would live to getting her well enough to come home. I was also worried about Glenn and how the stress of Mom's health was affecting his ability to tolerate dialysis. Quickly, life became so busy that, without realizing it, I forgot my own self-care and focused solely on the needs of my parents. My journal stayed tucked away in my bedside table for months, and my role as primary caregiver took precedence. It wasn't until years later that I finally understood the importance of self-care and realized that, without focus and attention to your own needs, you can be left with physical and emotional scars that will last well beyond the life of your loved one.

Guilt is one of those emotional scars that builds over time and can negatively affect your caregiving journey and relationships with other people. When you become a caregiver, guilt takes hold early on and often prevents you from asking for and accepting help. For instance, I had the growing feeling that family and friends had elevated me to a special status and that I had to meet their expectations. On more than one occasion, I was called a saint. I never felt that caring for my parents was worthy of sainthood. In fact, I felt that I was falling short in my role every day, which led to feelings of guilt and inadequacy. Along with these feelings, I was becoming emotionally drained and physically exhausted. But in spite of desperately needing help, it quickly became difficult to ask someone to step in and provide temporary care so that I could practice self-care.

It is important to note that while you are adjusting to your new role as a primary caregiver, you are also starting the process of grieving the loss of the relationship you had with your loved one—a relationship that has been replaced by that of patient and caregiver. There may also be added financial stress and feelings of isolation due to the loss of your own independence. These feelings are natural . . . **not** selfish. And that's because you are a caregiver, not a saint.

This book will walk you through my eight-year journey of caring for my parents and how, over time, I learned to manage the challenges that I was presented. I was blessed to have had a good relationship with my mother and stepfather. However, over the years I have met caregivers who cared for a friend or family member with whom they had a less-than-perfect relationship. Stepping into the caregiving role doesn't come with a magic formula that suddenly eliminates difficulties from the past. In fact, the opposite is true. Those challenges often magnify, and as the caregiver, you begin to feel guilty for having natural responses to past hurts.

At the end of every chapter, I have included unedited excerpts from my journals that show the feelings and emotions I struggled with while caring for my parents. I offer these, so you can see that you are not alone!

At the end of the book, I have included a workbook with writing techniques and suggestions to help you identify the source of feelings about the situations you are facing. The journaling techniques provided here come from a practice called Journal to the Self® and are offered to help you find better and healthier ways to express yourself. The journal along with self-reflection will help you navigate your caregiving journey in a more positive and emotionally healthy way. The JTTS techniques in this workbook can and should be used over and over since the same feelings will likely come up in different situations while you are caring for your loved one.

Throughout my journey, I used journaling to help with guilt, grief, anger, fear, love, and a myriad of other surprising emotions that I never could have anticipated. I now look back at those eight years of caring for my parents with happy, loving memories. And not only did I not make it to sainthood as a caregiver, but I don't expect to attain that title anywhere in my future. We are, after all, human.

PART 1:
MY JOURNEY

CHAPTER 1:

The Night That Changed My Life Forever

I REMEMBER IT like it happened yesterday. It was July 20, 2001, and the phone rang around 11:30 p.m. Picking up the receiver, I heard my oldest brother tell me something I could not comprehend at the time. "It's Mom. She is in UCLA! She had a massive stroke today, and they are not sure if she is going to make it." My head began to spin with questions and fear and an overwhelming need to be there . . . NOW. He said there wasn't a lot of information, but the doctors suggested family come as quickly as possible.

I hung up the phone and called my son, Michael. I needed to let him know about his grandmother and make a plan to get from Colorado to California. I told him what little I knew, and we considered if we should all go as a family. Since both my son and daughter-in-law work and my grandsons were in school, we agreed I would go alone until we had a better understanding of the situation. I hung up and made the arrangements for the trip that would forever change our lives.

I remember thinking almost immediately that I was going to do whatever it took to help my mom make it out of the hospital and return home. Although this was the beginning of my caregiving journey, it was not the moment that would determine my destiny. That had happened a decade before.

In my late thirties, I had moved from California to Colorado. My parents were retired and led very busy lives, but I still managed to speak with them every week. They traveled in their RV for weeks at a time, and when they were home, their lives were filled with community service and social activities. Trips to visit them were limited to a couple of times a year. As time went on and they started aging, I began to notice that Mom made it a point to schedule a doctor appointment or two while I was in town visiting. She wanted me to know about her health and to build a relationship with her medical team. She was very proactive about her health as well as the health of my stepdad. She even kept a medical diary where she logged her medical concerns. On one trip home, I teased her, saying that her record keeping wasn't necessary because she was going to live forever. She smiled and told me about a friend of hers who had suddenly become ill and suffered some permanent challenges that left her unable to take care of herself. Her friend's family made the difficult decision to place her in a long-term care facility. Mom was deeply troubled by the circumstance.

When she finished telling me the story, she looked me square in the eye and said, "Promise me you won't let that happen to us. PROMISE ME." And without hesitation, I made that promise. At the time, I had no understanding of the impact it would have on my life as well as the lives of my family members.

The truth is, we all expect our parents to age and understand that someday they will no longer be with us. But I never understood that there is more to aging than living and then dying. There is what I now call the gray area—the time in between. It begins when your parents age and they are less physically capable of performing tasks for themselves. Or when they begin struggling to make the decisions they had previously made on their own. In extreme cases, they can no longer manage the activities of daily living. Seeing your loved one struggle is difficult, and you may agree to take on the caregiving role without understanding the impact it will have on you and your family. Through my experience, I learned that it is important to understand the full magnitude and meaning of committing to this kind of promise. A deeper understanding may not change your mind, but it will help you make an informed decision.

Sitting beside Mom's hospital bed in the ICU, I listened as the doctors explained her odds of survival and gave pessimistic statistics about her quality of life. I remembered my promise. I made that when my parents were healthy and active, but now my stepdad was weak and frail from dialysis, and Mom was laying comatose in a hospital bed. I realized that keeping that promise was going to be a lot more difficult than I had ever imagined.

After a few days, the conversation changed from life or death to the reality of her survival—but not without serious physical challenges. The doctors felt Mom would never be able to live on her own and suggested we find a long-term care facility. Glenn took me aside. The look in his eyes was pure heartbreak when he said, "Please don't let this happen. She needs to come home. She can only get better if we are together." Remembering the promise I had made so many years before and seeing that desperate look in his eyes, I once again uttered the words, "I will make sure Mom comes home. I promise."

I felt torn as I thought of the comfortable life I would be leaving behind in returning to California to care for Mom and Glenn. Colorado had been my home for the past several years, and I had built a good life. My son and his family lived only a few minutes away. I had a good job and a support group of wonderful friends. I felt a kind of peace there that I had never felt in California.

But now there was a decision to be made. I called my son to discuss the situation, and without hesitation, he agreed I should move back to California to care for my parents for as long as they needed me. This wasn't an easy decision to make, but we both knew it was the right thing to do.

After that pivotal discussion with my son, I returned to Mom's bedside, took her hand, and simply said, "You're coming home Mom. I promise."

FROM MY PERSONAL JOURNAL

A Team to the End

I realize now it's you and me
A team to the end
You and me it will always be
Walking hand in hand

From my earliest recollection
A team we always were
Our relationship took directions
Before my birth for sure

Those Friday night game nights
We made a perfect team
Dad's disappointments out of sight
Your love made me beam

As I grew to teenage years
Our friendship grew and grew
At times causing you some tears
I hope only a few

Then came marriage much too young
In spite of your advice
Soon thereafter came a son
The light of our lives

It was you who helped me
To become who I am
Who puts first her family
Before herself and friends

I have tried hard to be
The best teammate to the end
I'll be here 'til God sets you free
Your loving daughter and best friend

CHAPTER 2:

The Road Home

THE ROAD HOME WAS NOT AN EASY ONE. Mom spent several days in intensive care and then another several weeks in the hospital, followed by eight weeks in intensive rehabilitation at UCLA Medical Center. During that time, I jumped right into my new role, spending eight to ten hours a day with Mom, meeting with doctors and rehabilitation therapists, and becoming acquainted with every inch of UCLA's long hallways and back corridors.

When I wasn't at the hospital, I was fulfilling Mom's role as Glenn's caregiver, which meant making sure he was eating properly, giving him medications, and driving him to Santa Monica for dialysis three days a week. Dialysis days were hard on him, so after his treatment, I would take him home to rest before bringing him to the hospital to visit Mom.

Those visits required several trips a day back and forth from my parents' home in Culver City to the UCLA Medical Center, which, round trip, took about two and one-half hours. In the evenings after

Mom had gone to sleep, Glenn and I would head back to Culver City where I would make sure he was comfortable before I did the necessary household chores like grocery shopping, laundry, meal preparation, and washing dishes.

Thinking back on those early days, I can now recognize the gradual loss of my identity. The medical staff began to refer to me as the *Primary Caregiver*, no longer by my name or as "Lupe's youngest daughter." I had willingly taken on this role and all of the responsibility that came with it, never recognizing that by doing so, pieces of myself were being lost to the persona that was beginning to form.

We were blessed to have Mom at a first-rate facility. The recovery team worked with Glenn and me and encouraged our step-by-step involvement in her rehabilitation. The stroke had left Mom paralyzed on her right side, so I learned the importance of always standing on her right side and directing her attention to the parts of her body that her brain no longer controlled. I learned to transfer her, shower her, and assist her with other daily needs like eating and dressing. And I worked with the rehab team to master all of the exercises I would be guiding her through at home.

The stroke also left Mom with expressive aphasia, meaning she could no longer use language to express herself. This presents differently for everyone, but in her case, she said the words *do do do* thinking she was saying full sentences. She would say, "Do do do," and wait expectantly for me to respond to her request. When I didn't immediately respond, she would become frustrated. So, I would tell her she just said, "Do do do," and she would look so surprised. Luckily, she was still able to understand language that was spoken to her, and on a random occasion, she could say a full sentence as if she had never had a stroke. Amazingly, she never lost the ability to say the words, "I love you," and over time, we found ways to communicate with each other effectively. However, this was not without trial, error, frustration, and a steep learning curve for both of us.

When Mom was finally discharged from UCLA Medical Center, I went into "get Mom better" mode. I honestly thought that she would make a full recovery. In my mind, there was no one in the world as strong as my mom. I steadfastly believed that within a year, she would be back on her feet, and I'd be able to move back to Colorado where life would continue just as smoothly and peacefully as it had before.

I was fortunate that in spite of Mom's strong and capable take-charge personality, she quickly realized that we needed to be a team in order to maintain a positive environment for her recovery. More importantly, she realized that I had to be the leader of that team. Like many caregivers, my life went from zero to one hundred miles per hour overnight. The calm and peaceful life I had worked so hard to create in Colorado now accelerated with fast-paced, around the clock caregiving.

Needless to say, caring for my parents took priority over every other aspect of my life. It became paramount to learn all I could about stroke and recovery for Mom's care and to become an expert on the needs of dialysis patients for my stepfather. In the evenings, I spent hours doing internet research to learn about new treatments and the latest groundbreaking medications.

I created a detailed care plan as suggested by the rehab therapists. Although their focus was on general aspects like medications and emergency information, I felt it was important to create a daily step-by-step guide so that nothing would be overlooked. I wanted to make sure that I maintained the full regimen of exercises and therapies that Mom was given. I compiled all of this information to create a daily plan that spelled out specific instructions on how to perform each task throughout the day.

The plan included:

- Transferring directions: It was important that Mom put weight on both feet, so I had step-by-step directions on how to transfer/move Mom from her bed to the wheelchair and from the chair to the toilet and back as well as in and out of the car.

- Daily grooming: Showering, dressing, makeup.

- Range of motion/endurance/walking exercises: These exercises were very important to make sure Mom's muscles did not atrophy and that she would retain the mobility that she had. These exercises were clearly listed as to when and how they should be performed.

- Bathroom breaks: Mom was on a schedule to avoid infections.

- Meal planning, including dietary instructions and allergies.

- Medication management: Over the years, Mom's daily medications varied from 14 to 20+.

And because Mom had difficulty communicating her needs, I even included information about her personal preferences for TV shows, snack times, etc., in anticipation of having future support from family and friends.

It didn't take long for the new schedule to consume our days. It seemed every waking hour was dedicated to Mom's new condition. Actually, caregiving found its way into my sleeping hours as well. In order to make sure I was aware if Mom needed anything throughout the night, I began sleeping with a baby monitor on my bedside table. It became a habit that would last for eight years. Some days I would awaken and realize I was holding my own breath, not allowing myself to inhale until I was sure I could hear her breathing first.

Slowly and steadily, my sense of self began to disappear, and I was so concentrated, so dedicated, and so overwhelmed in fulfilling my promise and upholding my new responsibilities, that I didn't see myself fading away.

Rather than waking up to a leisurely cup of coffee and half hour of writing in my journal, I now had to begin each morning with Mom's range of motion routine, so her muscles were limber enough to get out of bed. And this was just the beginning. Various needs extended into the length of the day. Subconsciously, I no longer thought of myself as anything but a caregiver. In many ways, I carry the residual identity with me today. Looking back, I now realize that if I had included self-care earlier as a part of the daily care plan, I would have experienced a much healthier caregiving journey.

If you don't have a care plan and want a place to begin, I have written a Daily Home Care Guide for the American Heart/American Stroke Association. You can find it on my website at www.CarePartnersResource.com/caregiver-resources. This guide is free and walks you through steps in designing your personal care plan.

The next page is a copy of the morning range of motion instructions I created for Mom's care plan. This was all performed before she was transferred out of bed each morning. The highlighted note at the bottom was directed to the hired caregivers that were later brought in.

LUPE'S DAILY ROUTINE

When Lupe wakes up in the morning, she likes to be rolled over onto her side for approximately 20 to 30 minutes.

- Roll her onto her left side.

- Take the pillow from under her feet and place it under her affected arm, making sure her arm is stretched out.

- Make sure her pillow is in a comfortable position.

When Lupe is ready to roll over, make sure she is on her back in a comfortable position. Now it is time to do some range of motion exercises. This helps with her flexibility and lessens her spasticity, so please make sure this is done properly every day.

- Take her right foot in your hands and stretch it toward her knee— slowly and not too far. This will help stretch out her tendon on the back of the foot. Then relax and repeat 3 to 5 times.

- Move the right leg into a bent position with her foot flat on the bed. Gradually stretch her leg open and over to the right as far as possible. Some days she can get close to touching the bed, but don't push too hard or too far; you will have to gauge based on her stiffness. Move back up and repeat 5 times.

- Let her legs straighten and let Lupe breathe and relax for a moment.

- The next exercise is to stretch her legs and back. Raise her right leg and take her left foot into your hands (I put her foot against my chest). Have Lupe bring her left leg up equal to the right and bend it toward her upper body.

- Bend both her legs with her feet flat on the bed. Hold her legs in place (lightly) then have Lupe lift her butt. Hold for the count of 5 and relax. Repeat 5 times.

- In the same bent leg positions, have Lupe roll her legs from the center to the right as far as she comfortably can. Then have her bring them back to the center. Then have her move to the left as far as comfortable and then back to the middle. Repeat this exercise 5 times. Be sure you support the legs, not allowing them to flop or wobble.

- In the same bent position, have Lupe resist while you try to pry her legs open, do this for a couple of seconds and repeat 5 times. Then, have Lupe open her legs as wide as she can and resist as you try to close her legs for 2 to 3 seconds. Repeat 5 times.

It is important to use good judgment in how many of these exercises you have Lupe do. You can do 2 to 3 daily and mix them up. The goal is to relax and stretch her muscles to make movement easier through the day. What we don't want is to exhaust her before she even gets up.

CHAPTER 3:

The *Culture of Caregiving*— What Happened to My Identity?

THERE ARE MANY REASONS A CAREGIVER begins to lose sight of their own needs and identity while caring for another person. It is important to realize that this is common, and you are not alone. I call this the *Culture of Caregiving*. Most caregivers understand that they need better self-care but have no idea where to begin or what it really looks like.

In my early days as a caregiver, I remember saying to myself, "This is my new normal. I need to learn how to manage this, and now is as good a time as any." So, I asked family and friends to please stop bringing food, and I refused to accept help in whatever form it was offered. Early on, my siblings offered what help they could as time allowed, but I now realize I pushed them away and always gave the impression I had everything under control. I felt that no one could really understand Mom and serve her needs in the way I could. Having to explain the care plan that I devised to anyone else took too long and felt like a waste of what little energy I had left. It was simply easier to do everything myself.

It didn't take long for the exhaustion to take hold. I began to resent the loss of my independence, but I also had this overwhelming feeling that I alone needed to provide the care. It took several years before I finally prioritized my own needs.

More often than not, caregiving becomes *who* you are instead of *what* you are doing. In other words, it defines your identity rather than describing your activities. This distinction is very important because when caregiving becomes your identity, even when you realize you are in need of self-care, asking for help feels like you are failing. But if you recognize that caregiving is something you are doing (an activity, like a job), then it becomes easier to ask for help. Everyone needs help sometimes in life, not just caregivers.

When the workload becomes too much or you are asked to do things beyond your capability, it's okay to take a step back and assess. For example, if you are not a medical professional and a doctor asks you to perform a medical task like giving a shot or inserting a catheter, it would naturally be okay to ask for help. I remember the first time the doctors told me I needed to give my mother shots of heparin in her stomach. I was immediately gripped with panic. Heparin is a very strong blood thinner, and the idea of sticking anyone with a needle, much less such a strong substance, made me very uneasy. However, I just looked at the doctor and said, "Okay." I didn't feel I had the right to assess the situation and express my discomfort. Since I had already taken on the caregiver persona, I felt that by not performing the task at hand, somehow, I was failing.

I felt as if I had graduated from high school on Friday, and on Monday, I had become the CEO of Mom's life. I had been handed this role with little training, yet I felt as though I needed to have all of the answers. Looking back, I realize that this made no sense! In the real world, in my job, I would speak up and ask for training. As a CEO, I would certainly need support to navigate the position, especially when encountering new situations, and I would likely delegate responsibilities, so I could focus on what I know best. However, once you take on the *Culture of Caregiving,* your persona becomes one of "the caregiver," and asking for or accepting help no longer feels like an option.

I did have one trusted companion, Tita, my mother's housekeeper and friend of more than twenty years. During the years I cared for Mom and Glenn, Tita became the only person I fully trusted with Mom's care. While I lived in California, she was my lifeline to sanity because she was able to step in at times, allowing me much needed periods to try and recharge. However, even when she relieved me, I was unable to completely relax because guilt and worry consumed me. I never felt fully replenished.

But many caregivers don't have someone like Tita to lean on. A common response when a loved one is in need of care is to take on the duties alone and to refuse help. After a while, managing the caregiving role alone becomes overwhelming. We feel stuck in the need to conduct daily responsibilities and then don't know how to reengage and relate to family and friends, feeling no one else can truly understand our experience. I'll be the first to admit I was wrong for pushing people away, but early in my caregiving, I was working with the information I had and could only make decisions based on how I felt and what I knew at that time.

My identity slipped away so gradually that I didn't even recognize it was gone. I was slowly growing more and more depressed but couldn't admit it to myself. And when feelings of guilt and anger would arise, I truly couldn't think of what would make the situation easier or better. A few years into my caregiving journey, I made a call to my therapist, Kay, and she encouraged me to pull out my trusted journal. With her guidance, I began to open up and allow myself to examine my feelings. By doing this I was able to recognize that I could no longer do it alone. With that realization, I was able to add self-care as part of the daily care plan . . . at least until the next crisis.

JTTS TECHNIQUE:
Character Sketch

WHO AM I NOW?

When I look in the mirror, I see a "caregiver"—not me any more. I see someone who has dark circles under her eyes and a smile that really doesn't reach those same eyes. I feel tired constantly. A deep down to my soul exhaustion that is hard to describe.

But I wear this mask that tells the world I'm fine. If you ask my family, I'm sure they would say I am so strong and that caring for Mom and Glenn hasn't phased me one bit. I get it all done every day. They only see the love that I feel for my parents and the duty that gets me through each day.

Most days I am okay, and every time Mom has a breakthrough or can do something new, it gets me through another day. And seeing the pride in Glenn's eyes when Mom is able to walk or write her name helps me moment by moment.

Yet I know I am no longer the same person as I was before I gave up everything and moved back home, and I wonder, will I ever be able to find her again? Do I need to? Do I want to? Only time will tell, but for now, I guess it doesn't matter who I am now. It only matters that I take good care of my parents because they took such good care of me.

CHAPTER 4:

Loss & Grief Lead to Advocacy

AFTER SEVERAL MONTHS of caring for my parents, life settled into a seemingly relentless routine: the grind of following a meticulous care plan, doing research on the subject of stroke survivor recovery, and attending several physical, occupational, and speech therapy or medical appointments each week. Mom's medical appointments became very repetitive and frustrating.

The doctor would ask Mom how she was doing. Mom would smile and say, "Do do do." And on the rare occasions when the doctors would turn to me and ask how everything was going, I would just shrug and say everything was *fine.* (The word *fine* was my new four-letter F word!) Looking back on that time, I'm sure the doctors were waiting for me to ask a question, any question that would help identify what it was that I needed.

The months turned into years, and the grind continued until January 18, 2003, when we suddenly lost Glenn to a heart attack. Mom was devastated, and her rehabilitation completely stalled. She had lost her reason to recover. Even though we were both in deep mourning, I managed to push my feelings aside.

I felt Mom's loss was greater than mine. I tried to find ways to help her through her grief and encourage her to regain her motivation for more recovery. Mom's doctor suggested increasing her antidepression medication, and initially, I agreed. I understood the value of grief therapy, but because Mom couldn't communicate her pain and grief with words, it never occurred to me to request a referral to a therapist. In hindsight, I wish one of her doctors had suggested professional help, but they never did.

After a few months of watching Mom sink deeper and deeper into what I thought was most likely depression, I sat down asked her some questions about what she was experiencing and made some suggestions to see how she wanted to proceed. We realized that she had not been allowed to go through the natural mourning process since the medication just kept her numb to her emotions. She wanted to be able to feel her loss and move through the grief.

So, I took on another important role as her advocate and spoke with her doctor about removing her from the antidepressant. It took some convincing, but he finally agreed. After a while, Mom began to move through her grief and return to her old self, filled with joy and once again motivated to work at her recovery.

As an advocate, it is important to work with your loved one's medical team. Yes, we'd like to think medical professionals are going to have all of the answers, but they are dealing with their own issues, like exhaustive workloads, multiple patients, insurance limitations, etc.

And remember, they may know *medicine*, but you know your *loved one*.

It's incumbent upon you as the caregiver to ask questions and investigate options. Ask about medications: what they do, their side effects, etc. Therapies—not only physical, but occupational, speech, and emotional—can be very helpful. Ask the doctor what your medical insurance will cover. And if it doesn't cover a certain type of therapy, find out if there are social service organizations in your area that can provide it free or at low cost.

This applies to not only emotional and physical health but also to questions you may have about home modifications. Your loved one's doctor is the first place to ask questions, get a referral, and seek advice. One suggestion: have your list of questions prepared for the doctor, and if it is lengthy, let the scheduler know that you need an extended appointment or consultation plus appointment. This way, they will be sure to schedule enough time, so you and the doctor aren't rushed.

JTTS TECHNIQUE:
Dialogue

SECRETS

Me: What is one of my secrets?

Secrets: You long for this caregiving part of your life to be over.

Me: No one, except Carla, knows the extent to which I desperately want to live only for myself and have this caregiving journey be over.

Secrets: What might happen if this secret were known?

Me: People would think much less of me.

Secrets: What good might come of it?

Me: Understanding, unburdening, the ability to cry.

Secrets: Think of someone who knows the public you. See yourself through this person's eyes. How would he or she describe you?

Me: Strong, sometimes hard businesswoman. Good sense of humor. Loving daughter, mother, and grandmother.

Secrets: What would an expert in human behavior put on a report?

Me:	This person is conflicted. While she loves this time spent with her mother and wants to keep promises she made, she is very sad and longs to live her life for the first time.
Secrets:	Imagine doing something you really truly love. What would it be?
Me:	Honestly, I can't think of a thing.
Secrets:	Well then maybe this is a good time to end our conversation, and I will let you think about it.
Me:	Okay. I am going to write about it and get back to you. Thanks for coming. May I reach out to you again?
Secrets:	Yes, I'll be here when you're ready to finish our conversation.

Feedback write:

Reading this, I am surprised by my worry of what people will think of me. I wonder if this is why I continue trying so hard to do all of this mostly alone. What is my problem with accepting help? I feel like I am so exhausted I can't even think or recall what I love to do. Is it because I don't remember or because I just don't even know who I am anymore? UGH!!!

CHAPTER 5:

Change Is Good?

GLENN'S PASSING made me acutely aware of how much I desperately missed my family and home in Colorado. I longed to live near my son, daughter-in-law, and grandchildren again. I had already missed almost three years of life events, and I didn't want to miss anymore. Also, I felt it important that the entire family be united in grieving the loss of my stepfather, the figure who had grounded and united us.

I spoke with my son, his family, and Mom about the possibility of moving back home to Colorado. What seemed like a simple solution created some turmoil. We had a family meeting and ran several scenarios. Mom could stay in the house in Los Angeles, and we would hire Tita to move in and care for her. She could move to a care facility near her home in Los Angeles (not my choice), or she could move with me to Colorado in order to be near my son and his family. Initially I struggled with even the smallest resistance, but it was an important lesson to learn about family dynamics and how they take on increased sensitivity when caregiving is involved.

Every member of every family, no matter what age, has their own set of needs, fears, and emotional scars from the past. We are all coming from our own perspectives and experiences. As a primary caregiver, I learned it's essential to recognize that behavior is often a result of fear when change and comfort are at stake. This was a difficult decision, and we needed to take a lot of factors into consideration to help Mom decide what was best for her future.

Mom had lived in Southern California for most of her life. This was where her team of doctors were, doctors we had come to know and rely upon. Most of her family and friends lived nearby, although many of her friends had faded away since her stroke. Moving to Colorado would mean leaving the home she had shared with Glenn for close to forty years. I knew that leaving the house would not be easy since so many memories and so much love had been shared there. After careful consideration, Mom conveyed her decision. She was very clear she wanted to come to Colorado with me. I was elated that Mom was willing to leave her past behind and put her trust in me and a new chapter.

Many caregivers must deal with situations in which their loved one is completely against moving locations, having to live with relatives, or being moved into a care facility. This is when it's important to seek outside assistance such as counseling or a Certified Senior Advisor. This is also where journaling can help you navigate the challenges and relationship dynamics you are facing.

In our case, after much discussion, our family was able to come together and agree on decisions about logistics and finances. We decided that Mom and Glenn's home would be sold, and she and I would move to Colorado where we would be close to my son, his family, and the friends I had there.

To my great relief, the move seemed to re-energize Mom. My son coached sports, and my grandkids played on various teams throughout the year. So, sports became a part of our lives that galvanized our social activities and time together. Mom loved sitting behind the backstop watching the games, and I loved being back in Colorado again.

I located new doctors, and after some discussion, they agreed to order physical, speech, and occupational therapy for Mom, so we could continue her recovery routine.

I thought doing some volunteering in Colorado might help Mom connect to her new community and feel productive and fulfilled. Before her stroke, Mom and Glenn had been avid volunteers for several local not-for-profit organizations. Given our new experience with medical conditions as a result of stroke, we chose the National Stroke Association whose headquarters were nearby in Denver. Mom helped with mailings, and I helped caregivers find resources. Together, we spoke to families in similar situations, sharing our story with the goal of teaching by example.

Mom seemed to enjoy going to the office, meeting new people, and being productive again. But after about a year, she began to slow down. Her recovery stalled, and her health began to slowly decline. It became clear that she preferred staying home, shopping, or lunching at her favorite Mexican restaurant. Eventually she stopped coming, and at the same time it became clear to me that working outside the home provided social interactions I had been missing. I enjoyed the work I was doing, and speaking with other caregivers helped me to realize that I wasn't alone in the complex feelings and experiences of caregiving. I accepted a part-time job at the National Stroke Association and found an agency to provide part-time care for Mom.

However, as much as I thrived in my new position, I felt guilt for working. I secretly felt ashamed that it had been four years since Mom's stroke and that she had not made the full recovery I thought was reachable. And I questioned my decision to move her from the life she had known in California. Had it been selfish of me to have moved her from her familiar environment because of my personal need to be close to my son and grandchildren?

The incredible responsibility for Mom's well-being and constantly mulling over the decisions I had made led to overwhelming feelings of loneliness and isolation. These complicated feelings began to manifest themselves in unhealthy ways: overeating, overspending, drinking more alcohol than I normally would, and developing unhealthy relationships. At times, I felt incredibly frustrated and angry, which caused me to lose my patience with Mom, family, and friends, but I couldn't put my finger on what was wrong. I had the tools at my disposal to help me understand my feelings, but in the chaos of just getting through each day, it took months to recognize that I needed help.

Finally, I made an appointment to see Kay, and she encouraged me to start writing in my journal regularly. The process helped me identify the sources of those complex and uncomfortable sensations. I began to accept that the move was good because, in order for me to provide the best care for Mom, I needed to feel safe and be happy. I also began to understand that Mom's recovery was not in my hands alone, and I had to accept her fate and forgive myself for mistakes I had made along the way. I realized that, moving forward, it was important to remind myself what I needed for self-care and try to practice it regularly.

Self-care isn't easy for most people, but it can be especially difficult when you're caring for a loved one because of the personal sacrifices and the deep and complex relationships that are involved.

There are a lot of reasons that caregivers put their needs last. In my case, it was guilt. It felt wrong to worry about what I needed or wanted when my parents had suffered such drastic changes in their lives. Journaling helped me recognize that it was okay, in fact necessary, to allow myself to feel natural human emotions and to understand that uncomfortable feelings are not only natural but necessary in our journey to be whole, honest, and self-accepting. I had to start by identifying what I truly needed from other people in order to feel cared for and supported. I had to allow myself to become comfortable asking for and accepting the appropriate help.

Although writing in my journal was a safe place to work through guilt and anger, I would write for a while and then become so overwhelmed by my daily responsibilities that I would stop and tuck my journal away until the next crisis. During periods of extreme stress, I would reach out to Kay and journal sporadically until I felt better.

I did not make journaling a regular habit until the year before my mom passed away. I had fallen into the *Culture of Caregiving*, feeling overworked, anxious, and fundamentally unworthy of self-care. Sadly, I hadn't let myself journal regularly even though I knew deep within that it would have been helpful. I've since come to understand that journaling works best as an ongoing program of maintenance like yoga, exercise, or prayer. That said, even sporadic journal writing can be very beneficial during your caregiving journey.

Once I was able to truly identify and accept my feelings, I found healthier ways to express them. For example, I began to recognize that my exhaustion was showing up as anger, so I made a point to allow myself a rest period during the day. The grief I felt over the loss of the mother-daughter relationship that I had cherished began to heal, and I started seeing my caregiving role as a gift rather than a burden. The guilt I felt for attempting self-care was never fully eliminated; however, I realized that my self-care could be practiced in short intervals, which lessened the degree of guilt I experienced. Shorter intervals away from Mom also made my time outside the caregiver role more fulfilling and ultimately beneficial. Eventually, I began to feel more comfortable leaving Mom in the care of our paid caregivers for longer periods of time to pursue my work and make new friends.

JTTS TECHNIQUE:

5-Minute Sprint

CARING FOR ME

Today I really need silence. Peace and quiet have been missing in my world for so long. From the moment Mom wakes up until I hear her remote click off late in the evening, there is noise. The TV, music, phone calls, helpers . . . constant noise.

If only I had a few minutes a day of quiet, so I could think or breathe. Noise makes my shoulders rise and rise until sometimes they feel higher than my ears. I feel the anxiety grow as the day continues. I don't blame Mom; all she has is her TV. It brings her joy, yet the volume is so high, I want to cry.

Feedback exercise:

Reading this, I feel an awareness of some of my anxiety. This is a simple thing to solve, so I wonder why I haven't thought of it before. Tomorrow I am going to go out and buy one of those things Mom can wear and hear the TV in her ear, so we can set the volume lower.

CHAPTER 6:

Back to Work

LIFE AT HOME HAD SETTLED into an easy routine. Mom was now 83 years old, and our energies became more focused on her comfort and happiness than her recovery. I had two reliable caregivers with whom Mom was happy and comfortable, which allowed me to begin a better practice of self-care. In doing so, I realized that I needed to feel valuable outside of the home too.

As luck would have it, the National Stroke Association saw an opportunity for me to use my caregiving experience and knowledge in their organization. My part-time work turned into a full-time position. My role changed from caregiver's advisor to a coordinator working in the education department. All of the programs that were being developed were created to educate hospital professionals about stroke survivors. Some of the staff members and I realized that caregivers needed more information and resources, not only regarding day-to-day practicalities, but for their own emotional and psychological well-being.

After some discussion and planning, my position changed again, and I started working more closely with programs designed specifically for caregivers. I helped create the National Stroke Association's *Careliving Community*, an online support group. On this website, caregivers are able to communicate with other caregivers, ask for advice, and develop online support by sharing information and establishing new friendships.

While developing and monitoring the *Careliving Community* site, I realized that I wanted to do more to help caregivers navigate the challenges of caring for a loved one. Since the day Mom came home from rehab, I would tell her that she survived her stroke for a reason, and when we began working with the National Stroke Association, we both felt that reason had become clear: it was to help survivors and their caregivers understand that there is hope after a devastating health crisis. We offered our journey as inspiration to others.

I also knew that I struggled in the early stages of caring for my parents and had come far in my journey. I wanted to take that knowledge and help others learn to manage the challenges of caring for a loved one while maintaining a practice of self-care. In honor of my mom and my journey, I created Care Partners Resource.

Perspectives Write—
One Year from Today

GOING BACK INTO
THE WORKFORCE

It has been a year since I took my job with the National Stroke Association, and I can see how much better I feel. I didn't realize how badly I needed to be back in the workforce. I am beginning to feel secure in this new industry, and I can see that I really am a positive contribution to the needs of caregivers.

Mom seems to be thriving by having more interaction with the other caregivers, and it is allowing me to go back to being her daughter rather than always her caregiver.

I had so many fears and doubts about taking this position, but now I feel that I did the right thing. Mom and I are better for it, and I am moving forward.

CHAPTER 7:

Saying Goodbye

TAKING CARE OF MYSELF came pretty late in my caregiving journey. As I began to grow in my new career, Mom was beginning to slow down. We had a couple of health scares that required hospitalization. During one stay, she was seen by an intern who suggested we consider putting her in hospice care. At first, I was enraged. Mom wasn't close to dying, so why was this young doctor giving up on her?

What I didn't realize was that she had begun having CVA's (cerebrovascular accidents), which were the cause of her recent decline. Once I shared this information with my siblings, we all felt a sit-down with her medical team was in order. I made an appointment, and the entire family—some in person and some via telephone—met with Mom and her medical team, including a hospice professional, so we could get an understanding of her prognosis.

During this meeting, we realized that she was not going to improve, and the condition was affecting her quality of life. The medical team explained in detail all of the benefits hospice would offer both Mom and our family. Mom listened carefully and thoughtfully, and it was clear she was ready to make the move to in-home hospice care.

The next day, Mom was discharged to home hospice. The following week, we were visited by a social worker, a nurse, a Certified Nurse Assistant (CNA), and a chaplain, all of whom were amazed at Mom's clarity of mind and physical strength in spite of her recent diagnosis. Each one of them commented that Mom was doing amazingly well and that she would probably be with us for a very long while. They said they were looking forward to caring for her through the final phase of her life journey.

But in the end, Mom had a different plan. On July 19, 2009, not a week into her hospice stay, I went into her room to find her weak and a little disoriented. She wanted to get up and shower, but while attempting to go through her grooming routine, it was clear that her physical capabilities were failing. Mom and I agreed it would be best to put her back in bed until she felt better.

Within half an hour, it became obvious that something very serious was happening, so I called my son to come quickly. Then, I called the hospice nurse. I was sitting next to Mom who was lying in her bed. I had the phone to my ear and could hear the nurse giving me some sort of instructions, but my focus was on Mom. I was talking to her and saying everything was going to be okay. I told her Michael was on his way. Thinking back, I'm sure this was more for my comfort than hers.

Mom was holding my hand tightly, and the look on her face was one of peace. She was looking over my shoulder. To this day I swear she saw Glenn and was ready to go with him. Her mouth turned up into a soft, beautiful smile, and she squeezed my hand harder. Then she closed her eyes and was gone. It was the most peaceful, beautiful thing I have ever experienced.

My son arrived only seconds later. I met him in the garage and told him that his grandma was gone. He went in to sit with her for a moment and then he called for the rest of the family who arrived shortly after. A while later, the hospice nurse and chaplain arrived to take care of all of the necessary details, which allowed us to sit with her in her room for what felt like several hours saying goodbye. It was the closure we all needed.

When Mom had her stroke, it felt like my life went from zero to 100 miles per hour. Then just like that, she was gone, and my life had gone back to zero. Who was I now if I was no longer a caregiver? I was about to find out.

JTTS TECHNIQUE:
Unsent Letter

DEAR MOM

What I've been wanting to tell you is thank you for being you. I am so grateful to have been blessed to have been your last child. Truly that was the lucky spot in the family of five kids. At the time we were young, you struggled financially and worked so hard to keep your head above water. Coming later, I got the best of you as you were older, had a better job, and fewer kids at home. Finally, when you met Glenn, I was the last one home, and you were able to stop working.

I also want to thank you for your grace. I am so sorry that you had your stroke, and yet I am grateful for it at the same time. It not only brought our family together for the time you were here, but it allowed me to move back home and find my way. In your difficulties I was able to find my way.

I found patience that, until then, I had no idea was in me. I found my calling: working with caregivers and helping them through the challenges of their new lives.

Most of all, it allowed us to spend eight beautiful years together. I was able to take care of you the way you did for me my whole life.

I have wanted you to know how much I miss you, but I also want to ask if I am holding you back from completing your journey. Is my need to constantly feel your energy near me keeping you and Glenn from being free? If it is, I want to say, Go ahead. Go and be free and experience your afterlife together—and as you need it to be. I will miss you, but I also know I will be with you again.

I see you off swimming with dolphins, no longer the stroke survivor who lost movement and speech, but freely moving joyfully and speaking clearly, full of energy and happiness.

Before you go, I want to tell you that I love you. You are my blessing, and I miss you, but I think I am ready to let you go.

This write helped me to see that it is okay to set you and Glenn free. I am okay and ready to move on.

CHAPTER 8:

Life Goes On

MY WORK AS AN ADVOCATE was a great blessing as I began rebuilding my life after caregiving. Because being a caregiver had come to define my identity, I felt lost when I no longer had that role to fill. My website and advocacy work had developed into a very important part of my life. Aside from helping caregivers find resources and manage the challenges of their journeys, offering them a way to find positivity or meaning in their situation became a large part of my work. The truth is, if Mom hadn't become a stroke survivor, I would not have become a caregiver's advocate.

Today my work has grown beyond my website to a YouTube channel where I co-host *Caregivers Tuesday Talks Outside the Box* and teach JTTS caregiver self-care workshops throughout Colorado in partnership with the Colorado Respite Coalition, a program of Easter Seals; Latino Age Wave; the Denver Art Museum; Denver Libraries; Colorado Area Agencies on Aging; the Alzheimer's Association; and the Parkinson Association of the Rockies. I have also created an informational video series for AARP that informs caregivers of varied resources. I think of my parents each and every day, hoping that they are proud of where our journey has taken us.

If you are a current caregiver reading my story, I hope you come to realize you are human, not a saint, and that forgiving yourself for the mistakes you have made is a first step in finding ways to incorporate self-care into your daily experiences.

Captured Moment

FEELS LIKE OUR "OLD MOM"

Today is Christmas Eve, and the family is beginning to gather. Here in Colorado and since Mom had her stroke, Christmas Eve has been much quieter than in previous years. This year I am determined to have an old-time family celebration filled with food, lots of people, and lots of love.

Mike, Carla, and the kids show up early bringing bags of gifts and some food. I am in the kitchen cooking and preparing our traditional Christmas Eve meal of meatballs for sandwiches, German Potato Salad, a meat & deli tray, and Mexican Wedding Cookies. The house smells of the Italian sauce for the meatballs that have been cooking all day.

The mood is light, and happy kids are sitting with Mom and Carla. Mike is helping set up the tables. This year we have friends dropping in, which adds to the fun.

At one point Carla is sitting with Mom, and she looks over at Carla and says, "Isn't this nice? Just like Christmas should be." Forgetting Mom's stroke, Carla begins having a conversation with her just like the old days. As we listen, the room fills with love and happiness. If only for a moment, we have our "old-mom" back.

PART 2:
THE WORKBOOK

THE FOLLOWING PAGES explain Journal to the Self® techniques, which can be used as a workbook to identify natural and human responses to emotions and feelings that may be evoked while caring for a loved one. The goal of the workbook is to offer techniques that may help you gain a deeper understanding of your responses and find solutions to the everyday feelings in the context of caregiving. These feelings might include anger, grief, regret, guilt, and frustration as well as happiness, joy, and contentment.

This workbook will guide you through seven of the eighteen JTTS techniques. Each technique includes a title, an explanation of the process, and an exercise that could be used in response to a specific feeling.

WHY JOURNALING AND WHY JOURNAL TO THE SELF®?

Journal to the Self® was created in 1985 by Kathleen Adams LPC, PTR, and Director of the Center for Journal Therapy, Inc., an internationally known pioneer and expert in the power of writing to heal. Nearly 100,000 people around the globe have learned this easy, effective, and empowering model of journaling.

Most of us are familiar with keeping a journal or writing in a diary. You may have tried some form of writing but found it difficult to make it a consistent, daily habit. When caregiving, doing anything regularly can seem impossible due to the daily unknowns and your loved one's changing needs. The JTTS techniques help you graduate from logging daily activities to expressing the honest feelings you are experiencing, including those that you aren't comfortable speaking out loud or sometimes even admitting to yourself. The process helps you examine the way you truly feel and consider information that will lead to healthier actions.

The goal here is not only to identify and process pent-up feelings but to clear the space to make your caregiving experience more manageable. In this way, caregiving becomes less of a burden, and you are more fully available to your loved one's care without subconscious emotions of resentment, anger, or loneliness. Consistent journaling will also help you accept appropriate help without experiencing guilt and the deep fear that you are falling short. It is also important to recognize that this workbook or the regular practice of JTTS techniques is not a substitution for professional care. It is entirely probable that in your writing, deep emotional issues may be brought to the surface, and in such cases, I recommend seeking professional help.

GETTING STARTED*

As we begin the workbook section, you'll see how JTTS techniques and the important feedback writes are designed to help you gain a better self-understanding. Here are a few things to keep in mind:

1. **Something to write in:** Everyone has a different preference when they write: a journal, a notebook, a computer, or even a phone app. Use what works for you.

2. **Choose a writing utensil:** It is helpful to have a pen or pencil that feels comfortable to write with, however not everyone has a preference.

3. **A time to write:** Finding "me time" may be a challenge. I wrote either in the morning before Mom woke up or in the evening once I put her to bed. Another option is to find a time when your loved one is busy. For example, when my mom was watching one of her favorite programs, I could step out onto the porch and journal.

4. **Safe storage:** When writing for any kind of self-discovery, you may touch on feelings you didn't know were there. It is important to be honest and not censored in your writing. This is not an easy thing to do, especially if there is fear that your journal could be found and read. Find a safe place (in a closet, underwear drawer, under the mattress, etc.) for storage. You can also write on the first page: *These are my private thoughts, please do not read!*

5. **Let one person know:** Some people worry, *If anything happens to me, what would happen if my loved one finds my journal?* If you have those concerns, pick someone who you trust and let them know where to find your journal; then make an agreement on what to do with it. Some may want part or all of it read; some may simply ask that it be destroyed. If you do not have anyone that you want to ask, you can add to your note on the first page: *If anything happens to me, please destroy and do not share the writings from this journal!*

Following the precautions in steps four and five will help you write from a deeper place.

6. **Find a comfy place to sit.** Settle into your chair, couch, blanket . . .

7. **Date every entry.** It's a great way to gauge your progress.

Adapted from the teachings of Kathleen Adams Journal to the Self®

PREPARING TO WRITE

This may feel strange to begin with, and that is okay. It is normal. As Kay Adams would say to me in our sessions, "No one is grading or judging you here. This is your journal; these are your feelings; there are no rules." Before you write, take a moment to acknowledge that this is your unique journey, and there is no perfect way to be a caregiver. You are taking a big step toward improving your caregiving experience by taking the time to write your feelings.

- Each technique has a suggested time limit. The shortest is the **5-Minute Sprint**, and the longest is the **Dialogue** at a 30-minute suggested time, each ending with a two- to three-minute feedback exercise (see next bullet).

- Use a timer to remind you when to put down your pen. Once the timer goes off, finish the sentence you are working on and put your pen down. You may not be finished—that is OKAY. Just finish your sentence and get ready for the next step. The words you have written while journaling will be referred to as your "write."

- The feedback is a very important part of the process. It takes you to a deeper understanding of your original write. Set your timer for two or three more minutes. Read your first write and then write an observation beginning with one of these three sentences:

  - I am surprised by _____.

  - I didn't realize that _____.

  - Reading this I feel _____.

- With each technique, try not to sensor your pen. Write swiftly and let your thoughts flow. Do not correct your spelling or worry if your handwriting changes or becomes messy; this is your subconscious expressing itself on the page.

- Prompts given for each technique are only suggestions to help you start your write. Feel free to use any of the suggested prompts or use one of your own to delve into your specific personal needs.

THE TECHNIQUE:
5-Minute Sprint

JTTS Description:

This technique is the quickest and simplest of all journal techniques. It's great for caregivers because it doesn't require a lot of time. This is a free-write process that begins with a question or a feeling that is on your mind. Write quickly and do not stop until your timer has gone off.

Benefit:

This technique can be used for a daily journal check-in on your emotional well-being. The **5-Minute Sprint** can assist in letting go of pent-up feelings and subconscious emotions of resentment, anger, or loneliness and eventually create an environment where you may be more open to accepting appropriate help without experiencing guilt.

Time:

Five minutes with a two-minute feedback exercise.

EXERCISE:
Self-Care. What Do I Need?

You may be struggling with self-care because the day-to-day needs of your loved one have taken precedence over your own. Self-care is important, and letting your needs go unmet can lead to burnout, anxiety, depression, or other serious health problems.

The **5-Minute Sprint** is an excellent technique for discovering what *you* need. Once you can identify specific needs and name them, you are taking steps toward self-care. It could be something as simple as a five-minute break on the porch to breathe in some fresh air, fifteen minutes to do some stretching or yoga, or an uninterrupted phone conversation with a friend.

Starting with just a few minutes a day will bring increments of well-being, and slowly but surely, you will find it easier to give yourself permission to work self-care activities into your day. By starting slow, you'll see that your loved one has not suffered from your self-care time, which helps you become increasingly more comfortable taking care of yourself. This in turn lessens the feeling of guilt. Over time, most caregivers find it easier to allow others to help and even step away for a few hours of self-care.

Prompts:
- Use one of the prompts below to begin your write.

- Today I need _____.

- If I had ten minutes to myself, I would _____.

- One thing I love doing for myself is _____.

- When I feel overwhelmed, it would help _____.

Remember to set your timer and end with the feedback exercise.

_____

_____

_____

_____

_____

_____

_____

_____

_____

_____

EXERCISE:
Resisting Assistance

In the last section, you followed writing prompts to help you determine what you need for self-care. Understanding what you need is an important first step. Asking for and accepting help is the next step. Some caregivers find it difficult to accept help for a myriad of reasons: guilt for taking "me time" when your loved one is sick and suffering, worry that your loved one's needs won't be met in your absence, and fear of judgment from family and friends. If you have completed the previous writing prompt and are still having difficulty asking for or accepting help, use this **5-Minute Sprint**. Perhaps the prompts below will give you a better understanding as to why you are resisting help.

Prompts:

- Use one of the prompts below to begin your write.

- Asking for help feels _____.

- When I accept help _____.

- Leaving my loved one in the care of anyone else is _____.

- Why do I resist letting others help?

- I can reengage family and friends by _____.

Remember to set your timer and end with the feedback exercise.

_____

_____

_____

_____

_____

_____

_____

_____

_____

_____

_____

EXERCISE:
Feelings of Frustration, Anger, Sadness, Guilt, etc.

It is not uncommon for caregivers to feel frustration, anger, or sadness for many reasons. The pressures and anxieties of day-to-day caregiving can lead to pent-up emotions that end up expressing themselves in surprising ways, and at times in ways that may leave your loved one feeling hurt or upset. Such incidents tend to leave you feeling guilty.

The **5-Minute Sprint** can help you identify why you are feeling sad, frustrated, or quick to anger. Understanding the difference between your loved one's intentions and your triggered reactions is key in healthy caregiving. You may have a situation that evokes sadness and catches you off-guard. It could be that you are actually experiencing the grief of the loss of the relationship you had with your loved one prior to caregiving. If you experience anger, it could actually be that you are not sleeping well and are short on patience. Feelings of frustration may result because you are still attempting to relate to your loved one as you had before they required your caregiving. The **5-Minute Sprint** technique can help you understand the triggers that are causing the emotions, so you can move toward "your new normal."

Once you can identify the "why" of your reactions, your self-awareness will lead to an ability to take a deep breath, pause, and avoid a loaded trigger response. Self-awareness will make for a better caregiving journey for all involved.

Prompts:

- Use one of the prompts below to begin your write.

- I become frustrated when _____.

- Sometimes I feel _____ when _____.

- I become angry when _____.

- Why do I get angry/frustrated/sad/ _____ [pick one or fill in the blank] when _____?

Remember to set your timer and end with the feedback exercise.

_____

_____

_____

_____

_____

_____

EXERCISE:
Grief

Caregivers deal with grief from a variety of losses associated with the relationship that once existed. In most cases, caregivers don't realize they are grieving at all. Logic dictates that since our loved one is still here and alive, we should be grateful, not grieving.

But sensations of grief can be caused by many sources. It may be the loss of the parent-child relationship in which the caregiver was accustomed to seeking parental advice and support. Perhaps the caregiver is grieving the loss of independence and freedom. Maybe they had to move to a different city to care for their loved one, and they are grieving the loss of the home or friends they had.

Using the **5-Minute Sprint** can help you identify your grief and work through your feelings.

Prompts:

- Use one of the prompts below to begin your write.

- Reading that grief can be experienced while my loved one is still here, it occurs to me that _____.

- What have I lost since I began my caregiving journey?

- Since caring for my _____, I miss _____.

- I think I am grieving the loss of _____.

Remember to set your timer and end with the feedback exercise.

_____

_____

_____

_____

_____

_____

_____

_____

_____

_____

_____

_____

THE TECHNIQUE:
Perspectives Write

JTTS Description:

With a **Perspectives Write**, you can step into the future or the past, resolve interpersonal differences with compassion, and glimpse the world as it might have been for you or as it might be for another. It is a process of altering your personal reality—your worldview—to consider another perspective.

A **Perspectives Write** can be a valuable tool in the decision-making process. By fast-forwarding in time and space, it allows you to write from the point of view of having already made a particular choice.

Benefit:

Writing from the perspective of the future—as if a particular choice has already been made—is a helpful way to visualize an outcome and develop comfort before implementation.

Time:

Ten minutes with a three-minute feedback.

EXERCISE:
Asking for or Accepting Help

The **5-Minute Sprint** helps you figure out your reason for resisting assistance. The **Perspectives Write** is a great exercise to ease you into the next step of actually asking for or accepting help. By placing yourself in the future and writing about how it feels to reach out for help or to say yes when help is offered, you are exploring the situation as if it has already happened, and you discover that it is not as fearful as you expected.

By writing as if you have asked for and received help, you create an understanding that your loved one can be cared for without your presence. If by chance you do write about something less positive, it can help you anticipate a potential problem and resolve it before it happens. For instance, you might write a scenario where your loved one's medication was missed or where they fell while you were away. The scenario has made you aware of a subconscious worry that is now in your consciousness. Take a moment to make sure the medication plan or fall hazard are addressed in your care plan, and before leaving, take time to review the care plan with the relief caregiver.

Prompts:

Use one of the prompts below to begin your **Perspectives Write**. Date your page with the suggested future date (e.g., three, four, six months).

- The first time I asked for help was difficult, but for the past three months, I have reached out to _____ and _____.

- For the past four months I have _____, and it feels _____.

- It has been six months since my loved one has been going to adult day care once a week, and _____.

- Last year, I started taking one hour a day to _____ and _____.

Remember to set your timer and end with the feedback exercise.

_____

_____

_____

_____

_____

_____

_____

_____

EXERCISE:
Creating a Care Team

Over time, using the **Perspectives Write** to imagine a care team can help you determine the individuals in your life that you can count on. This technique will also enable you to begin thinking about steps toward organizing the supportive team your loved one needs. Imagining the future three, six, or twelve months from now allows you to anticipate how it will feel to have built a care team. Seeing a positive future in writing is beneficial because it instills hope for positive change. Writing about the process of building your care team illuminates the notion that people in your life are willing to help or that by incorporating professional resources as a part of your care plan, you have more freedom to practice self-care.

A natural concern caregivers express is leaving their loved one under someone else's care. Writing from the perspective of the possible future may reveal that allowing others to help can be beneficial for you and your loved one.

You may find initially that you experience feelings of anxiety and guilt, but by writing from the future, you can imagine and develop creative and positive ways to allow family, friends, or professionals to offer support and help. Surprisingly, you may learn that delegating responsibilities such as shopping, bill paying, or house cleaning will provide you a needed respite. Self-care comes in many forms. And delegating also provides a space for others in your life to feel good about their ability to support and demonstrate their love and care.

Prompts:

Use one of the prompts below to begin your write. Again, it is helpful to date the page in the future.

- Six months ago, I built my care team of _____.

- A year ago, I asked _____ for help, and since that time, _____.

- It has been three months since I let go of some chores, and I _____.

- Last year I began building my care team, and for the past nine months I _____.

Remember to set your timer and end with the feedback exercise.

_____

_____

_____

_____

_____

_____

EXERCISE:
Having a Family Meeting

All too often, I hear stories from caregivers of rifts that develop with family members or friends during the process of caring for their loved one. Sadly, this occurred in my family. Conflicts usually arise when the primary caregiver experiences frustration due to expectations of others that are not being met. It can also happen when family or friends provide unsolicited input that is not productive and therefore becomes unwelcome.

Unfortunately, these situations often create feelings that go either unexpressed or communicated in a way that leads to hurt or negativity, leading to the boiling point of anger. These complex feelings can lead to serious intra-family conflicts and feuds. Sometimes such dynamics can carry on for years and develop in a manner that is seemingly irreparable.

Having a family meeting to productively discuss these challenges can open the door for better communication, define boundaries, and heal wounds. However, many caregivers express fear or resistance to planning such a meeting because the caregiver fears judgment or criticism. The situation might also be a breeding ground to unearth previously unspoken family grudges.

A **Perspectives Write** can help the caregiver imagine a future family meeting in a productive and thoughtful way. The process allows you to create imagined dialogue, organize your thoughts, and make lists of specific items that must be addressed. It can help you to internally organize your thoughts around sensitive issues like money, which may have created difficult family discussions in the past. Anticipating this difficult discussion is helpful in developing a productive agenda based on fact rather than emotion. In some cases, it may be helpful to bring in a professional who is skilled at moderating family meetings. On my website, www.CarePartnersResource.com, you will find talking points for holding a family meeting as well as a link to help you find a skilled professional.

Prompts:

Use one of the prompts below to begin your write. Again, it is helpful to date your page in the future.

- When we had the family meeting six months ago, it helped to _____.

- It's been a year since we met as a family to discuss _____, and since that time, _____.

- Three months ago, when we had the family meeting, _____.

- I am so grateful that we had a professional during our family meeting because _____.

Remember to set your timer and end with the feedback exercise.

_____

_____

THE TECHNIQUE:
The Unsent Letter

JTTS Description:

The **Unsent Letter** is a marvelous tool for what Kay calls the Four C's—Catharsis, Completion, Communication, and Clarity. Letters can be used for expressing deep emotions such as anger, grief, and love. They are also tools for gaining closure and insight. And they are an effective way of communicating your opinions, deepest feelings, hostilities, resentments, affections, or controversial points of view in a safe, nonthreatening manner.

The trick to the **Unsent Letter**, of course, is: don't plan to send it! This gives you permission to write without censorship, risk, or fear of hurting someone else. Kay says, "If after writing your letter you decide that you want to share what you've written, you are certainly free to do so. But writing with the knowledge that it is initially for your eyes only allows you to tell the complete truth faster."

Benefit:

Caregivers have many interactions with their care recipient, family, friends, doctors, therapists, coworkers, and more. At the same time, they are managing stress, life changes, and difficult emotions. The **Unsent Letter** is helpful to unblock the path for clear and concise communications by offering the caregiver a written way to voice and acknowledge their feelings, which will help to maintain healthier relationships.

Time:

Ten to fifteen minutes with a three-minute feedback.

EXERCISE:
Writing to Family or Friends about Unmet Expectations

Like many caregivers, I experienced the feeling of deep disappointment in others who I had hoped would step forward and provide the support I needed. I had expected certain people in my life to help with the care of my parents. It did not take long to realize that not everyone's idea of helping was the same as mine. Over time, I inwardly built resentment toward some individuals that I found impossible to voice, and that clouded my perspective and changed my feelings toward them.

By writing an **Unsent Letter**, I was able to come to terms with the fact that, in some cases, my expectations were simply unrealistic. At times I had wanted and asked people to do things that they felt incapable of doing. But I was unable to productively express my frustration and hurt, and they were unable to express their fear and anxiety. So, our relationship dynamics changed. Those individuals simply distanced themselves from me and my mom.

Writing an **Unsent Letter** to each individual who had not met my expectations allowed me to release some of my anger and resentment and understand that not everyone was as comfortable as I was in performing the hands-on activities Mom required. This revelation helped me devise a more productive way of asking for help with Mom's day-to-day needs. I would present a list of daily activities and allow family members or friends to pick a task they felt comfortable in executing. This allowed them to feel that they were participating in caregiving and allowed me to receive some needed support.

Prompts:

Use one of the prompts below to begin your write.

- Dear _____,

- I am writing today to _____.

- There is something I need to express_____.

- Since I began taking care of _____, I have felt that you _____.

- I want you to know _____.

Remember to set your timer and end with the feedback exercise.

_____

_____

_____

_____

_____

EXERCISE:
Writing to Your Loved One

Caring for a loved one comes with a mixed bag of emotions, some positive and some challenging and even negative. Challenging and complex emotions can eat away at you when you carry them inside with no release.

Without careful monitoring, it's natural to misdirect the anger you feel toward your loved one. But in an **Unsent Letter**, you can write down all of your misdirected, confusing, and complex emotions and release them from your mind in a private and productive manner. By getting them out on the page, you may discover that your anger is actually directed to the disease rather than your loved one or toward your loved one's actions in not better monitoring their health. Perhaps your relationship prior to caregiving had been strained, and those emotions are now rising to the surface. Discovering a new perspective can allow you to redirect your feelings, forgive your loved one, and in the process, forgive yourself for having misdirected your emotions.

Prompts:
Use one of the prompts below to begin your write.

- Dear _____,

- I am writing today because I am feeling _____.

- I need to express how angry I have felt that _____.

- I'm writing because I have become so _____.

- This current situation feels _____.

Remember to set your timer and end with the feedback exercise.

_____

_____

_____

_____

_____

_____

_____

_____

_____

_____

EXERCISE:
Writing an Unsent Letter to the Disease, Your Fate, or Life in General

In the previous exercise I encouraged you to write an **Unsent Letter** to your loved one to help you better understand the cause of your complex and challenging emotions. Feeling angry and frustrated at the reason you have become a caregiver is a natural response to an unwelcome situation. It is perfectly valid to write an **Unsent Letter** to the emotions or situations that are the source of your current circumstance (the disease that caused your loved one to become ill, or life itself if you feel you've been dealt a rough hand).

Prompts:
Use one of the prompts below to begin your write.

- Dear Anger, Life, Cancer, Dementia, etc.

- I am writing today to let you know _____.

- I need to tell you _____.

- I'm writing because I feel _____.

- Why have you _____?

Remember to set your timer and end with the feedback exercise.

_____

_____

_____

_____

_____

_____

_____

_____

_____

_____

_____

_____

_____

_____

THE TECHNIQUE:
Character Sketch

JTTS Description:

A **Character Sketch** is a written description of another person or yourself. It's a very useful technique when you're having a conflict with someone, when you want to see how you might be coming across to someone else, or when you want to get to know the different parts of yourself more directly and intimately.

Benefit:

This technique allows the caregiver to take a step back from their interactions and see them from the perspective of others. This new perspective can create awareness that might not otherwise be apparent.

Time:

Ten minutes with a two-minute feedback exercise

EXERCISE:
Checking in on You

When caring for a loved one, it may become difficult to assess your psychological and emotional health from day to day. The **Character Sketch** technique is a great way to step outside of yourself and gain insight into how you are managing all of your caregiving responsibilities.

Investigating how someone else may perceive your interaction with your loved one can provide insight on your performance. You can determine success and areas where you might want to improve. Did that person perceive you as patient and understanding? Did you engage with a sense of assurance, so they felt safe and secure? Were there moments when you were short, impatient, aggressive, or lost in your own thoughts? If the **Character Sketch** reveals any of the latter behavior, it's a good indication that you might be over-scheduled or in need of a break to provide yourself time and space for self-care.

The goal here is not to create guilt or chastise yourself for poor performance, but to assess areas of concern. Often, this kind of write can remind you of the deep compassion and skills you are bringing to your role as caregiver.

Write a **Character Sketch** from the perspective of a person who witnessed your interactions with the loved one you care for. It might be a clerk at the grocery store or a waiter at a favorite restaurant.

Prompts:

Use one of the prompts below to begin your write.

- Today I checked out a person who was caring for a loved one, and I noticed_____.

- While working my shift today, I observed _____.

- I had a patron at one of my tables today who _____.

- There is a couple who visit our restaurant often. One is ill, and the other is the caregiver. Today I noticed _____.

Remember to set your timer and end with the feedback exercise.

_____

_____

_____

_____

_____

_____

_____

THE TECHNIQUE:
Dialogue

JTTS Description:

Kay refers to the **Dialogue** as the Swiss Army Knife of the journal toolbox. She says, "It is a marvel of flexibility that can take you into or through nearly any journal situation you can imagine."

Dialogue is an exchange between you and someone or something else, where you imagine and write both sides of the exchange. In the journal, a **Dialogue** is a written conversation. On the page, it looks like a movie or theater script.

Benefit:

Subconsciously, **Dialogue** allows you to write your way through a difficult conversation that opens the door to a deeper understanding of what you are trying to convey.

As an example, you may be upset with your loved one who is now on dialysis due to years of ignoring proper nutrition even after receiving a diagnosis of diabetes. Your hope is to get them to make positive changes in their habits. Engaging in this conversation without properly formulating your thoughts and feelings could erupt into an exchange of accusations leaving everyone feeling angry or hurt. Preparing for this conversation by using the **Dialogue** technique will help you find productive ways to express your feelings.

It is important to remember that if you are dialoging with a force in your life that isn't serving you in a positive way, it's a good idea to end your **Dialogue** by asking that thing to move on.

Example: Dialogue with Anger

| Me: | It has been twelve years since Mom passed |
| Anger: | I know. |

| Me: | Why are you still here? |
| Anger: | Because you need me. |

| Me: | For what? |
| Anger: | So, you don't allow doctors to miss health issues with you or your family like what happened to your parents. |

| Me: | My work has taught me to advocate for myself. |
| Anger: | What does that mean? |

| Me: | It means that while I appreciate you wanting to help me, I don't like how you make me feel. |
| Anger: | I'm just trying to be helpful. |

| Me: | I appreciate that, but I need you to go away so I can heal. |
| Anger: | Okay. I didn't mean to cause you pain. |

| Me: | Thank you. I've got it from here. |

Time:

Twenty-five to thirty minutes with a three-minute feedback

EXERCISE:
Discussion with Your Loved One

Caregiving comes to each of us differently. Some have a clear understanding when making the decision to care for a loved one. Others, like me, agree to the role without fully grasping the sacrifices involved. An illness or occurrence that causes a loved one to become physically or mentally incapacitated adds to this complex relationship.

Whether you are caring for someone for whom you have the most love and respect or a person with whom the relationship has experienced ups and downs, caring brings its own set of challenging feelings and emotions, which may not be appropriate to voice directly to your loved one. **Dialogue** provides a great way to speak your truth.

Prompt:

Below is an example of the beginning of a **Dialogue** write to help you get started. Remember, you are making this up, and it may or may not represent a real conversation.

Me: I want to talk to you about something.
Loved one: Okay, what's on your mind?

Me: I feel like when I try to plan healthy meals, you get upset.
Loved one: I don't get upset, but I like certain foods.

Me: I know, but some of those foods have contributed to making you sick.

Love one: Well, it's my life.

Me: But your decisions have now affected my life because ...

Remember to set your timer and end with the feedback exercise.

_____

_____

_____

_____

_____

_____

_____

_____

THE WORKBOOK

EXERCISE:
Anger, Resentment, Grief, Life...

Earlier in the **Unsent Letter**, I suggested you write to the disease, your fate, or to life, even though writing to one of these things might feel odd.

Similarly, having a **Dialogue** with your negative emotions may feel uncomfortable. But dialoguing can help you gain a deeper understanding of your actions and the manner in which you are responding to the needs of your loved one as well as the people in your life affected by the circumstance. A **Dialogue** with grief might create an awareness that you have begun to distance yourself emotionally from your loved one in anticipation of their passing. Or, a **Dialogue** with resentment may help you to recognize that because you resent the current situation, you feel less empathy for your loved one, so you have less patience.

Prompt:
Below is an example of a **Dialogue** write to help you get started.

Me:	I really don't understand why you keep showing up.
Grief:	It must be because I'm on your mind.
Me:	What do I have to grieve about?
Grief:	I can think of a lot of stuff, but right now, are you thinking about the future?

Me: No, I don't want to think about that.

Grief: Well, I really think it's on your mind, so I keep coming to see if I can help your feel better.

Me: How will talking to you about that help?

Remember to set your timer and end with the feedback exercise.

_____

_____

_____

_____

_____

_____

_____

_____

_____

THE TECHNIQUE:
Captured Moments

JTTS Description:

The **Captured Moments** technique allows you to celebrate and savor, preserving the pleasure and pain of your life. It is a frozen morsel of time. **Captured Moments** are best written from the five senses. This technique allows you to pull out all the stops with your creativity, describing in detail the sounds, sights, smells, and feelings of a moment in time and space.

Benefit:

The **Captured Moments** technique does simply that: it allows you to re-create a specific moment in writing. Day-to-day experiences of a caregiver are busy and complex, which makes it challenging to always be fully present in the moment. A **Captured Moment** is an excellent way to preserve special moments in writing.

Time:

Seven minutes with a two-minute feedback exercise.

EXERCISE:
Lessons

During your caregiving experience, you will or may have already had times that were so difficult, you weren't sure you had the strength to continue on. However, you did make it through!

By using the **Captured Moments** technique, you will relive the experience and by doing so, come away with a new understanding of your own strengths, abilities, and achievements. The beauty of this is that you can learn from past challenges and become better equipped for the next time a similar situation occurs. Remember, there are aspects of your life that go beyond caregiving, and the things you learn about yourself can be applied to all areas and relationships.

Prompts:

Use one of the prompts below to begin your write. (Remember to write from all your senses and be detailed about where you were, what you wore, an odor or scent in the air, or even the weather—these details help capture the moment.)

- One of the hardest days of caregiving so far was the day when _____.

- I learned so much from the time_____.

- My proudest moment as a caregiver came from the time

_____.

- I remember when _____.

Remember to set your timer and end with the feedback exercise.

EXERCISE:
Memories

Caring for a loved one comes with its share of challenges and struggles, however there are happy times too. **Captured Moments** is an excellent technique for preserving some of the positive, funny, and happy moments that are shared. When I was caregiving, I kept a special journal specifically for this purpose.

One of my favorite funny memories came unexpectedly. It was the Thursday before a long weekend, and my part-time hired caregiver had four days off. In preparation, I was going to run errands and go grocery shopping. Mom and I were discussing the menu when I asked, "What do you want for dinner on Saturday?" She looked at me and casually responded, "Sex," to which I burst out laughing. Mom was momentarily horrified and then began to laugh as well. When we regained our composure, I looked at her, smiled, and said, "Well the best I can do is brats." To that, we laughed until we cried. To this day, recalling the scene of us sitting at the kitchen table with tears of laughter streaming down our faces brings me great joy.

Although caregiving can be challenging even on good days, there are great gifts that come from being a caregiver. This teaches us that we are capable of things we never thought possible and illuminates our own human capacity to experience and share love.

Prompts:

Use one of the prompts below to begin your write. (Remember to write from all your senses and be detailed.)

- One of the most special memories I have while caring for _____ was when _____.

- I always smile when I think of that day _____.

- My favorite moment so far has been _____.

Remember to set your timer and end with the feedback exercise.

_____

_____

_____

_____

_____

_____

_____

THE WORKBOOK

CONCLUDING
REMARKS

WOW I think I feel better already!

I HOPE THIS IS HOW YOU MAY FEEL after completing each writing technique. I wish I could tell you that by reading my book and completing each technique your stress and worry will permanently disappear.

But the truth is, the life of a caregiver is filled with experiences that change from day to day. My hope is that each time you read this book and complete a technique, it will help you cope with your next challenge in a healthier more satisfying way, ultimately improving your experience.

Caring for a loved one can be one of the best experiences of your life when you allow yourself grace and remember . . . YOU'RE A CAREGIVER, NOT A SAINT.

ABOUT THE AUTHOR

LORI RAMOS LEMASTERS, is the founder of Care Partners Resource, a website designed to assist family caregivers with the daily challenges of caring for a loved one. Lori was a Caregiver to both of her parents during the final eight years of their lives. She understands firsthand the life-altering choices that caregivers make every day. Since her parents'  passing, Lori became certified as a Journal to the Self® Writing Instructor and uses these techniques in educational workshops to support family and professional caregivers. Her work focuses on self-care education in order to help caregivers identify and understand the feelings of stress and burnout that can come while caring for a loved one.

Lori has partnered with organizations such as the Colorado Respite Coalition, a program of Easter Seals Colorado; the Seniors' Resource Center; the Alzheimer's Association; Parkinson's of the Rockies; Latino Community Foundations; Latino Age Wave Project; and the Denver

Art Museum, speaking to caregivers on the importance of self-care and the benefits of using a journal. Under the last names of Cavallo and Lemasters, Lori has published many articles for the American Heart & Stroke Association's *Stroke Connection Magazine* and the National Stroke Association's *Stroke Smart Magazine*.

She recently created and co-hosted three caregiver videos and hosted eight *Care-FULL Conversations* for AARP. With Nadine Cornish Roberts of Caregivers Guardian, Lori co-hosted *Caregivers Tuesday's Talks Outside the Box*, which can be viewed on the Care Partners Resource YouTube page. Lori is trained in Patient Navigation by Boomers Leading Change in Health (BLCiH) and is certified from the Area Agency on Aging for Eden at Home and Project Visibility.

Made in United States
Orlando, FL
02 June 2023